PEGAN

SLOW COOKER
RECIPES

Paleo-Vegan Recipes

Rae Lynde

www.PeganPantry.com

Ordinary Publishing Matters

PEGAN SLOW COOKER PALEO VEGAN RECIPES:
Collection of 30+ slow cooker recipes for the Pegan diet
Ordinary Publishing Matters
OrdinaryPublishingMatters.com

DISCLAIMER: The recipes within this book, PEGAN SLOW COOKER RECIPES, are for information purposes only and are not meant as a diet to treat, prescribe, or diagnose illness. Please seek the advice of a doctor or alternative health care professional if you have any health issues you would like addressed or before you begin any diet.

Book Layout © 2014 BookDesignTemplates.com

PEGAN SLOW COOKER PALEO VEGAN RECIPES/ Rae Lynde--
1st ed.
ISBN: 978-1-941303-24-5
ASIN: B01CWPD7FA (ebook)

www.PeganPantry.com

www.facebook.com/PeganPantry

"No matter how old you are, no matter how much you weigh, you can still control the health of your body."

—DR. OZ

TABLE OF CONTENTS

WHY I LOVE PEGAN

Pegan. It's a strange-sounding word, isn't it? I know the first time I heard it in early 2015, I thought it was an odd name for a diet. After a little investigation, I found it is the result of bringing the best of two diets together: Pegan and Vegan.

For the confirmed Paleo and pure Vegan dietary adopters, I doubt this diet will fully satisfy either one. Because of the inclusion of meat, vegans will say this is not a truly inspired vegan diet. For avid Paleo dieters, there isn't enough meat. But for many people, the Pegan diet is a wonderful pathway leading to a healthy and flexible dietary lifestyle.

In this book you will receive an introduction to the Pegan Diet, a quick outline of its rules and restrictions, as well as the thirty plus mouth-watering

Pegan Diet slow cooker recipes. (I love the ease of one-pot meals, don't you?)

The Doctors and the Pegan Diet

The Pegan Diet hit my radar when I stumbled across one of Dr. Oz's shows in May of 2015 when he had Dr. Mark Hyman on his show to talk about the various health benefits of his newly coined Pegan diet, especially when dealing with inflammation issues.

The Pegan Diet minimizes risk. Gone are the added sugars, dairy, gluten, processed foods, refined oils, and heavy reliance on meat. All of them contribute to inflammation. So if you want to reduce inflammation, go Pegan. If you want to reduce stress, adapt your eating habits to conform to the Pegan lifestyle.

A Quick Look at Healthy Pegan-style Eating

The Pegan diet is simple and easy to follow. The core idea is to increase vegetables and decrease meat. Dr. Hyman also advocates that you move toward a diet that is gluten-free and dairy free. The emphasis is on eating right. Add more sources of protein like nuts, seeds, eggs, and fish. Try to eliminate as much sugar as possible and monitor much of you eat when it comes to grains and beans.

Reduce your Meat Intake

For Dr. Hyman, meat is a "condi-meat." That's his way of describing how you change the way you look at meat. For most people, the meat portion is the main portion. In the Pegan diet, meat is a condiment or window-dressing. The goal is to lower the meat intake, while upping the vegetable consumption.

For me, this is a natural dietary lifestyle. I don't metabolize meat as fast as other foods so I gain weight when I eat heavy meat-laden meals. The pounds drop off as soon as I switch back to my more natural dietary habit of eating more vegetables and less meat.

For most vegans, this is the most controversial aspect of the idea of combining Paleo and Vegan diets. No animal fats is the mainstay of the vegan diet. True vegans will not embrace this diet. But for those who appreciate the vegan and vegetarian lifestyle but prefer to ensure that they have some meat in their diet, Pegan is a good option.

Embrace Clean Meat

Dr. Hyman embraces the idea of clean meats, those that offer the best of animal protein. "All meat is not created equally," says Dr. Hyman. Most of us recognize the truth that increased cholesterol and inflammation is a product of most meat that is bought at the local grocery store due to hormones, chemicals, etc... The better meat is grass fed.

From his research, Dr. Hyman explains that "eating sustainably raised, clean meat, poultry and lamb and other esoteric meats such as ostrich, bison or venison" leads to much healthier, beneficial results such as the following:

- Increases good cholesterol (HDL)
- Increases testosterone and muscle mass
- Lowers blood sugar
- Reduces appetite
- Reduces belly fat
- Lowers triglycerides

In short, go for quality not quantity, and in the process you will realize that you don't need as much meat in your diet as you think.

Choose your Beans Wisely

Any vegetarian or vegan will sing the praises of beans. Most of us know their benefits, but do we understand how to control our intake to make sure we consume them in a way that will help us and not cause unintended consequences?

As Dr. Hyman has rightly suggested--and Dr. Oz concurs--beans are our friends but the amount eaten daily should be confined to no more than one half cup.

While beans are a great food, not everyone digests the same. In addition to their fiber and protein, it's good to remember that they are a starch and can put weight on you. In addition, as a starch their intake should be monitored by diabetics.

One good way is to make good choices. Eat small beans like lentils and stay away from the larger beans. You'll have less and feel much better.

Watch your Grains

Grains are good for you. A half cup of cooked low-glycemic, gluten-free grains per day are best. Black rice and quinoa are two great grains that you should definitely consider adding to your diet and are top grains for the Pegan diet. You will find terrific health benefits for both.

Resume your Friendship with Eggs

Unless you have strict dietary rules about eggs, feel free to add them to your Pegan diet. Full of protein and choline, eggs are definitely a plus food. New studies have liberated the egg. Eggs offer many healthy benefits, so do add them to your diet. The new guidelines now permit everyone to eat the complete egg and not simply the whites.

Focus on Small Fish Rich in Omega 3

Again, you may have your reasons why fish is not in your diet, but for those who love fish, wild salmon and sardines are two that work well with the Pegan diet. You have less to worry about when it comes to the mercury content in fish. These fish are also high in omega 3 fat and great for your brain.

What I like about the Pegan diet is that it combines principles from both the Pegan and the Vegan or Vegetarian diets. In truth, I have found that I gravitated naturally toward a similar diet and found it to be effective when it comes to achieving healthier goals such as a reduction in blood pressure as well as in losing weight. I, too, have found that reducing my intake of animal fat helps me to become much healthier.

Wean yourself Off from Dairy and Gluten

Today more and more people, either by choice or necessity, are moving towards dairy and gluten-free diets. Many make the choice due to the health benefits they receive when they eliminate these foods.

Gluten-free breads, crackers, and even cake mixes are easily found in most grocery stores. Dairy-free products are also more easily discovered, too. Almond milk, coconut milk, and many other dairy-free milk substitutes are available.

Instead of focusing on what you can't have, spend more time learning about all the wonderful foods you do have that will enhance your life and your health.

THE PEGAN DIET

Struggling to lose weight? Looking to improve your health? The best thing you can do is to improve your dietary habits.

Going on a diet doesn't necessarily mean that you have to count calories or severely restrict yourself; it simply means that you are altering your eating habits for the better.

There are countless different diets out there; however, so many people find the task of choosing a diet overwhelming. As I've said, if you are looking for a diet with proven health benefits that is also easy to follow, the Pegan Diet is a terrific choice.

The Paleo - Vegan Connection

The Pegan Diet is a combination of two very popular diets – the Paleo Diet and the Vegan Diet. The Paleo Diet is based on the eating habits of our Paleolithic-era ancestors and it includes only those foods which would have been available prior to the birth of agriculture. This diet includes fresh eggs, seafood and meat, fresh fruits and vegetables, nuts and seeds, avocado and olive oil, herbs and spices. The Paleo Diet excludes things that require processing or refinement to make edible, such as dairy products, grains and legumes. The Vegan Diet is free from all animal products which include eggs, meat, fish, seafood, honey, and dairy products.

Both the Paleo Diet and the Vegan Diet are based on the concept of whole food nutrition – that is, fresh and wholesome foods that have been minimally altered by man. The Pegan Diet is a combination of these two diets – it follows the rules of the Paleo Diet but restricts consumption of any animal product that would normally be included.

Five Health Benefits of the Pegan Diet

1) Rich in nutrients including vitamins and minerals

2) Low in antibiotics, hormones, and pesticides

3) Very low glycemic load (no grains or refined sugar)

4) High in healthy fats (avocado, olive oil, nuts, etc.)

5) May be lower in calories than standard diets

Eight Ways to Avoid or Reduce Animal Fat

The Pegan diet is not a vegan diet. Vegans seek to completely eradicate animal fat from their diet. In the Pegan diet you want to greatly reduce the level of animal fat that you take in on a daily basis. While I don't completely avoid animal fat, I do use a number of "vegan" products to help lower the amount of animal fat I consume daily.

Vegan-marked products are much more easily found in regular grocery stores than ever before. I often find these products in either the produce section, a natural or "whole foods" aisle or area, or in a special section in the cooler dairy area. You must find the word "vegan" on the container to make sure what you are buying is completely free of animal fat.

Here are some ways that I have successfully managed to make that happen.

1) Substitute "vegan" butter instead of the usual butter or margarine.
2) Substitute coconut oil for oils that contain animal fat.
3) Substitute "vegan" mayonnaise for the regular mayo you get from the grocery store.
4) Substitute avocado oil when coating a baked potato.
5) Substitute "vegan" sour cream for regular sour cream.
6) Substitute "vegan" cheese for your regular shredded cheese.
7) Eliminate all animal fat for one meal per day.
8) Have an occasional no-meat day.

What you Need to Do

If you think that the Pegan Diet might be the right choice for you, you will need to make some changes to your eating habits.

1) Clean out your kitchen and pantry of all processed grains, refined sugars, dairy products, and packaged foods.
2) Restock with fresh, wholesome foods like fruits and vegetables, nuts, seeds, and avocado.

3) Avoid gluten-containing grains and choose gluten-free grains like quinoa and black rice.

4) Choose low-starch beans and legumes like lentils.

5) Avoid dairy products.

6) Focus on eating mostly plant-based foods, though some grass-fed meats, fish, and seafood are allowed as well.

A Quick & Easy Beginner Pegan Pantry List

To help you get started in stocking your Pegan Diet pantry, choose from the following lists of foods to enjoy, eat sparingly, and avoid:

Foods to Enjoy Freely

Asparagus	Blueberries	Coconut yogurt
Avocado	Figs	Fresh herbs
Artichokes	Cantaloupe	Spices
Brussels sprouts	Honeydew	Broths/stocks
Broccoli	Lemon	Vinegars
Carrots	Lime	Walnuts
Cabbage	Mango	Pistachio
Cauliflower	Peaches	Almonds
Celery	Plums	Cashews
Eggplant	Pears	Flaxseed
Green onion	Watermelon	Chia seeds
Spinach	Strawberries	Sesame seeds
Kale	Oranges	Olive oil
Onion	Bananas	Avocado oil
Mushrooms	Grapes	Coconut oil
Bell pepper	Coconut milk	Almond butter
Zucchini	Coconut flour	Cashew butter
Apples	Almond flour	Baking powder
Blackberries	Tapioca starch	Baking soda

Foods to Eat Sparingly

Acorn squash	Brown rice	Molasses
Green beans	Buckwheat	Dried fruit
Peas	Lentils	Dark chocolate
Sweet potato	Dried beans	Cocoa powder
Pumpkin	Maple syrup	Grass-fed meats
Spaghetti squash	Agave nectar	Eggs
Potatoes	Dates	Fresh fish
Quinoa	Coconut sugar	Seafood
Wild rice	Fruit juice	

Foods to Avoid on the Diet

Wheat	Peanut butter	Ice cream
Barley	All-purpose flour	Frozen yogurt
Rye	Wheat flour	Vegetable oil
Couscous	Cake flour	Canola oil
Spelt	Cow's milk	HFCS
Triticale	Sour cream	White sugar
Corn	Cheese	Artificial sweetener
Oatmeal	Heavy cream	Honey
Soba	Half-n-half	
Peanuts	Cottage cheese	

Time to dive in and try the thirty delicious slow cooker recipes that follow.

Additional Notes

_____

_____

_____

_____

_____

SLOW-COOKING

The Pegan diet is perfect for anyone who loves slow-cooking methods. I love Crock-Pots, or slow cookers as they are often called. My history with crock pots begins back in the early 1970s when I bought my first Crock Pot. Loved it, and probably for all the reasons you do today. Nothing unlocks flavors like the cook low, cook slow method.

In this slow-cooker collection of recipes, you'll find recipes for breakfast, for main entrees, and for desserts that all fit in with the Pegan dietary guidelines.

A Little Slow Cooker History

Slow cooking is not new. There is evidence that clay pots were used over wood fires going back some six thousand years. While we may not have any of those ancient recipes, the cooking method is as useful today as it was necessary then.

Prior to the 70s many cooks relied on appliances like the electric bean pot, a simple ceramic pot that had a heating element that allowed you to cook beans all day, instead of using the stovetop.

The original modern crock pot was invented by Irving Naxon who received his patent in January 1940, and forever changed the landscape of home cooking. His Lithuanian grandmother was the inspiration for Nixon's slow cooker invention, when he learned of a dish of hers called Cholent that would be cooked overnight. His grandmother would take her pot of ingredients to the local bakery and use their oven. Naxon came up with the idea of using that "low and slow" method by putting the crock inside a heating unit. The cooks of the 1950s loved the idea.

The first big wave came in 1970 when Rival Mfg. bought Naxon's idea and produced the first, original "Crock-Pot." This classic appliance came in several colors of the day and even had its own cookbook. You'll find the classic pot roast as well as stews, chili, and curry. Want a good soup or a slow-cooked dessert? No problem. You'll find these slow cooker recipes to be a wonderful addition to your cookbook collection.

Why are Slow Cookers so Popular?

Convenience and flavorful cooking are the two main reasons modern cooks have embraced slow cookers. The original Crock-Pot hit the market at a time when women were entering the workforce in a major way. Slow cooking made it easy for a working mom to feed her family a delicious hot dinner at the end of a long work day. It seemed almost effortless.

In 1975 more than three million Crock-Pots found their way into homes. Even in the early 2000s, it was discovered that more than eighty percent of homes in the United States still owned a slow cooker. Why not? They are easy and definitely energy efficient.

Slow Cookers Today

Today slow cookers have come into their own. They are easy to use, easy to clean. The crock part is removable so portability has increased. If you have a slow cooker with a rubber seal and a lock, they make it easy to carry the food from one place to another. Some can even stir themselves and others come with automatic timers and temperature probes. Would you believe you can even buy one with a built-in Wi-Fi.

Benefits of Slow Cooker Cooking

There are three big reasons why today's cooks turn to slow cookers to prepare meals.

1) Easy clean-up
2) Ability to use less expensive meats
3) Convenient

What to Cook in a Slow Cooker

Slow cookers are used to create a wide variety of dishes from soup and beans, to stews, meat, and seafood, as well as vegetable dishes and desserts. Pot roasts are a staple. Families enjoy classic dishes like pot pies, chilies, stews, curries, and beans. It would seem you can pretty much slow cook anything you can imagine.

Thirteen Slow Cooking Tips

Here are thirteen things to keep in mind when you use a slow cooker.

1. More is not better. Don't stuff the food into the slow cooker thinking more is better. *Most slow cookers do best when filled to the two-thirds mark.*

2. Monitor your slow cooker when you first start using it on high and on low. You don't want to go away for hours only to return and find out the new cooker has a problem overheating.

3. Completely thaw frozen food before adding it to the slow cooker. Unless the frozen items are specifically created for slow cooker meals, you will increase the possibility for bacteria to grow.

4. Place your slow cooker on some kind of surface like a baking sheet, stovetop, or granite countertop because it does get hot.

5. Don't lift the lid to check on the food. You will only add more cooking time.

6. Don't stir the food. That will add more time to the cooking process.

7. For full flavor, brown the meat, especially ground meat.

8. You can also sauté the vegetables before putting them into the slow cooker. If you use flour to cover the meat before browning, you'll get a much thicker sauce.

9. Take advantage of layering, but make sure you put firm vegetables like potatoes and carrots on the bottom, and then add the meat. You'll get

better results if everything is cut up in equal sizes, too.

10. Wait to add any dairy products like yogurt, milk, or sour cream. Add them about fifteen minutes before you're ready to serve.

11. Cut the fat and the chicken skin. You don't want that oily, greasy taste.

12. Do not use any food that has been kept on warm or never cooked because you forgot to turn on the cooker. That creates a huge threat of bacteria. Better to throw the food out.

13. Instead of cutting a recipe in half, go ahead and make the full recipe and freeze the extra portion.

BREAKFAST RECIPES

Spinach and Red Pepper Frittata

Servings: 6

Ingredients:
1 cup frozen spinach, drained
1 large red bell pepper, cored and diced
1/2 small red onion, diced
9 large eggs, whisked well
Salt and pepper to taste

Instructions:
1) Squeeze as much moisture from the spinach as you can then transfer it to a mixing bowl.

2) Stir in the red pepper, red onion, and eggs – season with salt and pepper to taste.

3) Grease the insert of your slow cooker and pour in the egg mixture.

4) Cover and cook on low heat for 2 to 3 hours until the center of the frittata is set.

5) Remove the lid and let cool for 5 minutes before serving.

Nutritional Information:

120 calories per serving, 7.5g fat, 3g carbs, 10g protein, 1g fiber

Additional Notes

Use this section to make additional notes.

_____

_____

_____

_____

_____

_____

Butternut Squash Breakfast Stew

Servings: 6 to 8

Ingredients:
1/2 cup raw walnut halves
1/2 cup raw cashews, whole
Water, as needed
1 medium butternut squash, peeled, seeded and chopped
2 ripe medium apples, cored and chopped
2 tablespoons coconut sugar
1 cup canned coconut milk
1 1/4 teaspoon ground cinnamon
1/4 teaspoon ground nutmeg

Instructions:
1) Combine the walnuts and cashews in a bowl and cover with water – soak for 12 hours then drain.
2) Place the drained nuts in a food processor and blend into flour.
3) Combine the butternut squash, apples, coconut sugar and coconut milk in the slow cooker.
4) Stir in the ground nuts along with the cinnamon and nutmeg.

5) Cover the slow cooker and cook on low heat for 8 hours until the squash is very tender.

6) Mash the mixture with a potato masher and serve hot.

Nutritional Information:

270 calories per serving, 18g fat, 26g carbs, 5.5g protein, 5g fiber

Additional Notes

Use this section to make additional notes.

_____

_____

_____

_____

_____

_____

_____

_____

Sweet Potato and Egg Casserole

Servings: 8 to 10

Ingredients:

2 lbs. sweet potato, shredded

1 lbs. uncooked bacon, chopped

1 small yellow onion, chopped

1 medium red bell pepper, cored and chopped

12 large eggs

1 cup unsweetened almond milk

Instructions:

1) Whisk together the eggs and almond milk then set aside.
2) Cook the chopped bacon in a heavy skillet over medium-high heat until crisp.
3) Drain the bacon on paper towels.
4) Spread half the sweet potatoes in the slow cooker and sprinkle with half the bacon.
5) Add half the onions and red pepper.
6) Repeat the layers then pour in the egg and almond milk mixture.
7) Season with salt and pepper to taste, then cover the slow cooker.
8) Cook on low heat for 4 hours until the center of the casserole is set.

9) Uncover and let cool for 10 minutes before serving.

Nutritional Information:

420 calories per serving, 25.5g fat, 21.5g carbs, 26.5g protein, 3.5g fiber

Additional Notes

Use this section to make additional notes.

_____

_____

_____

_____

_____

_____

_____

_____

_____

Quinoa Porridge with Pecans

Servings: 6

Ingredients:

1 1/4 cups uncooked quinoa

3 3/4 cups unsweetened almond milk

5 pitted Medjool dates, finely chopped

1 large ripe apple, peeled and chopped

2 1/2 teaspoons ground cinnamon

1 teaspoon vanilla extract

Pinch salt

1/4 cup raw honey

1/3 cup chopped pecans

Instructions:

1) Combine the quinoa, almond milk and dates in the slow cooker.
2) Stir in the apples, cinnamon, vanilla extract and salt.
3) Cover and cook on high heat for 2 hours until the quinoa absorbs the liquid.
4) Spoon the quinoa into bowls and serve drizzled with honey and garnished with chopped pecans.

Nutritional Information:

340 calories per serving, 11g fat, 58g carbs, 7g protein, 7g fiber

Additional Notes

Use this section to make additional notes.

_____

_____

_____

_____

_____

_____

_____

_____

_____

_____

_____

Zucchini, Tomato, Basil Frittata

Servings: 6

Ingredients:
1 large zucchini, peeled and diced
1 large ripe tomato, diced
1/2 small yellow onion, diced
1/4 cup fresh chopped basil
9 large eggs, whisked well
Salt and pepper to taste

Instructions:
1) Combine the zucchini, tomato, yellow onion and eggs in a mixing bowl.
2) Stir in the basil then season with salt and pepper to taste.
3) Grease the insert of your slow cooker and pour in the egg mixture.
4) Cover and cook on low heat for 2 to 3 hours until the center of the frittata is set.
5) Remove the lid and let cool for 5 minutes before serving.

Nutritional Information:
125 calories per serving, 7.5g fat, 4g carbs, 10.5g protein, 1g fiber

Spiced Pumpkin Butter

Servings: 8 to 10

Ingredients:
2 (15-ounce) cans pumpkin puree
1 1/4 cups raw honey
1 1/2 teaspoons vanilla extract
1 tablespoon ground cinnamon
3/4 teaspoon ground nutmeg
1/2 teaspoon ground ginger

Instructions:
1) Whisk together the pumpkin, honey, and vanilla extract in the slow cooker.
2) Cover the slow cooker then cook on high heat for 4 hours or on low heat for 8 hours.
3) During the last hour of cooking, stir in the cinnamon, nutmeg, and ginger.
4) Crack the lid if you want a thicker consistency for your pumpkin butter.
5) Remove the lid and let cool to room temperature before spooning into jars to store.

Nutritional Information:
180 calories per serving, 0.5g fat, 47g carbs, 1g protein, 3g fiber

SOUPS AND STEWS

Beef and Bacon Chili

Servings: 6 to 8

Ingredients:
2 tablespoons olive oil
1 large yellow onion, diced
1 tablespoon minced garlic
2 lbs. lean ground beef
2 large carrots, peeled and diced
2 medium stalks celery, diced
1 medium jalapeno, seeded and minced
2 (14-ounce) cans stewed tomatoes
1 (14-ounce) can diced tomatoes
1 1/2 cups tomato sauce

3 tablespoons chili powder

2 teaspoons dried oregano

2 teaspoons dried basil

1 1/2 teaspoons ground cumin

Salt and pepper to taste

Instructions:

1) Heat the oil in a large skillet over medium heat.

2) Add the onions and garlic – cook for 4 minutes until the onion is translucent.

3) Stir in the beef and cook until evenly browned.

4) Drain the fat then transfer the mixture to a slow cooker.

5) Stir in the remaining ingredients then cover the slow cooker.

6) Cook on low heat for 6 hours until the vegetables are tender.

7) Serve hot garnished with chopped avocado and red onion.

Nutritional Information:

350 calories per serving, 13g fat, 17g carbs, 43g protein, 5.5g fiber

Turkey, Kale and Sweet Potato Soup

Servings: 6 to 8

Ingredients:

3 cups chopped sweet potato

1 large yellow onion, diced

2 medium stalks celery, diced

10 cups chicken broth

1 teaspoon poultry seasoning

1 1/4 teaspoon dried thyme

Salt and pepper to taste

3 cups cooked turkey breast, chopped

4 cups chopped kale

3 tablespoons balsamic vinegar

Instructions:

1) Combine the sweet potato, onion, and celery in the slow cooker.
2) Stir in the chicken broth, poultry seasoning and thyme – season with salt and pepper to taste.
3) Cover the slow cooker and cook on high heat for 4 hours or 8 hours on low.
4) Add the turkey and kale then cook on high heat for 1 to 2 hours until the kale is cooked.

5) Stir in the balsamic vinegar and adjust seasonings to taste.

Nutritional Information:

270 calories per serving, 4.5g fat, 26g carbs, 31g protein, 4g fiber

Additional Notes

Use this section to make additional notes.

_____

_____

_____

_____

_____

_____

_____

_____

_____

_____

_____

Butternut Squash Soup

Servings: 6 to 8

Ingredients:
4 lbs. butternut squash, peeled, seeded and chopped
1 medium yellow onion, chopped
2 large apples, cored and chopped
2 large carrots, peeled and sliced
1 teaspoon minced garlic
2 1/2 cups vegetable stock
1 teaspoon dried sage
1 1/2 teaspoons dried thyme
Salt and pepper to taste
1 1/4 cups unsweetened almond milk

Instructions:
1) Combine the butternut squash, onions, apples, carrots and garlic in the slow cooker.
2) Stir in the vegetable stock, sage, and thyme – season with salt and pepper to taste.
3) Cover the slow cooker and cook on low heat for 6 to 8 hours.
4) Whisk in the almond milk then puree the soup using an immersion blender.
5) Adjust seasonings to taste and serve hot.

Nutritional Information:

190 calories per serving, 1.5g fat, 44g carbs, 5g protein, 8g fiber

Additional Notes

Use this section to make additional notes.

_____

_____

_____

_____

_____

_____

_____

_____

_____

_____

Easy Beef and Vegetable Stew

Servings: 6 to 8

Ingredients:
2 tablespoons olive oil
3 1/2 lbs. beef stew meat, chopped
1/2 cup almond flour
Salt and pepper to taste
2 large onions, diced
1 1/2 cups sliced carrots
2 cups diced sweet potatoes
1 (6-ounce) can tomato paste
1 1/2 cups beef broth
1/2 teaspoon dried oregano
1/2 teaspoon dried thyme

Instructions:
1) Preheat the oil in a large skillet over medium-high heat.
2) Toss the beef with the flour and season with salt and pepper to taste.
3) Add the beef to the skillet then cook until evenly browned.
4) Transfer the beef to the slow cooker and stir in the onions, carrots, and sweet potatoes.

5) Stir in the tomato paste, beef broth and herbs – season with salt and pepper to taste.

6) Cover the slow cooker then cook on low heat for 7 to 8 hours or on high heat for 4 hours. Serve hot.

Nutritional Information:

575 calories per serving, 20g fat, 24g carbs, 73g protein, 4.5g fiber

Additional Notes

Use this section to make additional notes.

_____

_____

_____

_____

_____

_____

_____

_____

Smoky Split Pea and Ham Soup

Servings: 6 to 8

Ingredients:
2 lbs. ham hocks
2 1/2 cups diced carrots
2 cups diced celery
1 large yellow onion, chopped
1 1/4 lbs. split peas
5 (14-ounce) cans chicken broth
1 1/2 teaspoon dried thyme
Salt and pepper to taste

Instructions:
1) Place the ham hocks in the slow cooker.
2) Add the carrots, celery, onion, garlic and split peas.
3) Whisk together the chicken broth with the thyme and season with salt and pepper to taste.
4) Pour the broth into the slow cooker and cover it – cook for 7 to 8 hours on low or 4 hours on high.
5) Transfer the ham hock to a cutting board.
6) Let rest for 5 minutes then shred with two forks.

7) Stir the ham back into the slow cooker and serve hot.

Nutritional Information:

590 calories per serving, 18.5g fat, 50g carbs, 56g protein, 20g fiber

Additional Notes

Use this section to make additional notes.

_____

_____

_____

_____

_____

_____

_____

_____

Coconut Pumpkin Curry

Servings: 6 to 8

Ingredients:

2 1/2 cups pumpkin puree
1 (15-ounce) can full-fat coconut milk
1 1/4 cup chicken broth or vegetable broth
1 tablespoon curry powder
1/2 teaspoon ground turmeric
2 1/2 teaspoons garam masala
4 cups chopped sweet potatoes
1 large yellow onion, diced
4 large carrots, peeled and diced
2 teaspoons minced garlic
Salt and pepper to taste
Juice from one lime
1/2 cup fresh chopped cilantro

Instructions:

1) Whisk together the pumpkin, coconut milk, and chicken broth in the slow cooker with the curry powder, turmeric and garam masala.

2) Stir in the sweet potatoes, onion, carrot and garlic then season with salt and pepper to taste.

3) Cover and cook on low heat for 6 to 7 hours until the vegetables are tender.

4) Stir in the lime juice and cilantro then serve hot over steamed brown rice.

Nutritional Information:

280 calories per serving, 12g fat, 40g carbs, 5g protein, 8g fiber

Additional Notes

Use this section to make additional notes.

_____

_____

_____

_____

_____

_____

_____

_____

Sausage, White Bean & Collard Green Soup

Servings: 8 to 10

Ingredients:

3/4 lbs. andouille sausage, sliced

1 1/4 lbs. dried white cannellini beans

1 large yellow onion, chopped

3 medium stalks celery, chopped

9 cups chicken or vegetable broth

2 teaspoons fresh chopped thyme

Salt and pepper to taste

8 to 10 cups fresh chopped collard greens, stems removed

1 1/2 tablespoons red wine vinegar

Instructions:

1) Combine the sausage, beans, onion and celery in the slow cooker.
2) Stir in the broth and thyme – season with salt and pepper to taste.
3) Cover the slow cooker and cook for 7 to 8 hours on low heat or 4 to 5 hours on high until the beans are tender.
4) During the last 20 minutes of cooking, stir in the collard greens.
5) Stir in the vinegar then serve hot.

Nutritional Information:

575 calories per serving, 15.5g fat, 45g carbs, 63g protein, 15.5g fiber

Additional Notes

Use this section to make additional notes.

_____

_____

_____

_____

_____

_____

_____

_____

_____

_____

_____

Root Vegetable Slow Cooker Stew

Servings: 6 to 8

Ingredients:

2 tablespoons olive oil
2 large yellow onion, chopped
1 tablespoon fresh minced ginger
1 tablespoon minced garlic
1 teaspoon ground cinnamon
1/2 teaspoon ground coriander
Salt and pepper to taste
4 large carrots, peeled and chopped
3 large parsnips, peeled and chopped
2 medium sweet potatoes, peeled and chopped
3 cups vegetable broth
1 small butternut squash, peeled and chopped
1 (15-ounce) can chickpeas, rinsed and drained
4 cups chopped baby spinach

Instructions:

1) Heat the oil in a large skillet over medium-high heat.
2) Add the onions, ginger and garlic – cook for 4 to 5 minutes until the onions are translucent.

3) Stir in the cinnamon and coriander – season with salt and pepper to taste.

4) Spoon the mixture into a slow cooker then stir in the carrots, parsnips, and sweet potatoes.

5) Add the broth then cover the slow cooker then cook for 1 1/2 to 2 hours on high heat.

6) Stir in the squash and chickpeas then adjust seasoning to taste.

7) Cover the slow cooker and cook on high heat for 2 hours until the vegetables are tender.

8) Stir in the spinach and cook for 5 minutes until wilted – serve hot.

Nutritional Information:

465 calories per serving, 9g fat, 84g carbs, 18g protein, 20g fiber

DINNERS

Sausage and Cauliflower Stuffed Peppers

Servings: 6

Ingredients:

6 assorted bell peppers
1/2 head cauliflower, cut into florets
1 cup diced yellow onion
1 tablespoon minced garlic
2 teaspoons dried basil
1 1/2 teaspoons dried oregano
1 lbs. ground Italian sausage (sweet or hot)
1 cup tomato paste
Salt and pepper to taste

Instructions:

1) Slice the tops off the peppers then scoop out the seeds and membranes.
2) Place the cauliflower in a food processor and pulse until it forms rice-like grains.
3) Transfer the cauliflower rice to a mixing bowl and stir in onion, garlic, basil and oregano.
4) Cook the sausage in a large skillet over high heat until browned – drain the fat.
5) Stir the sausage and tomato paste into the cauliflower mixture and season with salt and pepper to taste.
6) Place the peppers upright in the slow cooker and spoon the sausage mixture into them.
7) Put the tops back on the peppers then cover the slow cooker.
8) Cook on low heat for 6 hours until the peppers are tender. Serve hot.

Nutritional Information:

320 calories per serving, 18g fat, 20.5g carbs, 17.5g protein, 5.5g fiber

Pecan-Mashed Sweet Potatoes

Servings: 6 to 8

Ingredients:

2 1/2 lbs. sweet potatoes, peeled and cubed
1 1/4 cup unsweetened apple juice, divided
1 tablespoon ground cinnamon
1 1/4 teaspoon ground nutmeg
1/4 teaspoon ground cloves
1/2 cup chopped pecans to serve

Instructions:

1) Place the sweet potatoes in the slow cooker and stir in 1/2 cup apple juice.
2) Add the cinnamon, nutmeg and cloves then cover and cook on low heat for 4 to 5 hours until the sweet potato is very tender.
3) Remove the lid and mash the sweet potatoes with a potato masher.
4) Whisk in the remaining apple juice then adjust seasonings to taste.
5) Spoon into bowls and top with the chopped pecans to serve.

Nutritional Information:

280 calories per serving, 7g fat, 52.5g carbs, 3.5g protein, 8g fiber

Additional Notes

Use this section to make additional notes.

_____

_____

_____

_____

_____

_____

_____

_____

_____

_____

Beef and Mushroom Bourguignon

Servings: 6 to 8

Ingredients:

2 lbs. beef stew meat, chopped

2 tablespoons almond flour

Salt and pepper to taste

2 tablespoons olive oil

1 large yellow onion, chopped

1 tablespoon minced garlic

2 cups beef broth

4 tablespoons red wine vinegar

2 1/2 tablespoons Dijon mustard

8 ounces sliced mushrooms

1 1/2 cups sliced carrots

1 1/2 cups diced parsnips

2 bay leaves

2 1/2 tablespoons water

2 tablespoons tapioca starch

Instructions:

1) Toss the beef with the flour and season with salt and pepper to taste.

2) Heat the oil in a large skillet over high heat – add the beef and cook until browned, stirring as needed.

3) Transfer the meat to the slow cooker and stir in the onions and garlic.

4) Add the beef broth, red wine vinegar, and mustard then stir in the mushrooms, carrots, parsnips, and bay leaf.

5) Cover the slow cooker and cook on low heat for 8 hours or high heat for 6 hours.

6) Spoon about 1 cup of the cooking liquid into a small saucepan and bring to boil.

7) Whisk together the water and tapioca starch then whisk it into the saucepan.

8) Cook for 1 minute, stirring constantly, then stir the mixture into the slow cooker.

Nutritional Information:

400 calories per serving, 17g fat, 16g carbs, 44.5g protein, 4g fiber

Spaghetti Squash and Meatballs

Servings: 4 to 6

Ingredients:

2 cups tomato sauce
1/4 cup roasted red peppers, drained and chopped
2 tablespoons olive oil
2 tablespoons minced garlic
1 teaspoon dried basil
1/2 teaspoon dried oregano
1/2 teaspoon dried thyme
1 large spaghetti squash
1 lbs. ground Italian sausage (sweet or hot)
1 small yellow onion, diced

Instructions:

1) Combine the tomato sauce, roasted red peppers, olive oil, garlic and herbs in the slow cooker.
2) Cut the spaghetti squash in half and scoop out the seeds.
3) Place the squash halves cut-side-down in the slow cooker.
4) Combine the sausage and onion in a mixing bowl then shape into small meatballs.

5) Add the meatballs to the slow cooker around the squash.

6) Cover the slow cooker then cook on low heat for 5 hours or high heat for 3 hours until the squash is very tender.

7) Remove the squash and shred it with two forks.

8) Stir the squash back into the sauce and serve hot with the meatballs.

Nutritional Information:

265 calories per serving, 15.5g fat, 19.5g carbs, 15g protein, 2g fiber

Additional Notes

Use this section to make additional notes.

_____

_____

_____

_____

_____

_____

Vegetable and Chickpea Curry

Servings: 8 to 10

Ingredients:

1/2 tablespoon olive oil

1 large yellow onion, chopped

2 medium sweet potatoes, peeled and chopped

Salt and pepper to taste

1 tablespoon curry powder

1 tablespoon coconut sugar

1 tablespoon minced garlic

1 inch fresh grated ginger

2 1/4 cups vegetable broth, divided

2 assorted bell peppers, cored and diced

1 medium head broccoli or cauliflower, chopped

2 (14-ounce) cans diced tomatoes

1 cup canned coconut milk

1 (10-ounce) bag frozen spinach

Instructions:

1) Heat the oil in a large skillet over medium heat.

2) Add the onions and cook for 5 to 6 minutes until translucent then stir in the sweet potatoes.

3) Season with salt and pepper to taste and cook for 5 minutes.

4) Add the curry powder, coconut sugar, garlic, and ginger – cook for 1 minute.

5) Stir in 1/4 cup broth and cook for 2 minutes.

6) Transfer the mixture to a slow cooker and stir in the remaining ingredients aside from the coconut milk and spinach.

7) Cover the slow cooker and cook on high heat for 4 hours.

8) Add the coconut milk and spinach, stirring well, then cover and cook for 5 minutes or until the spinach is wilted.

Nutritional Information:

175 calories per serving, 8g fat, 23g carbs, 5g protein, 5.5g fiber

Chicken and Mushroom Pot Pie

Servings: 4 to 6

Ingredients:

1 1/2 lbs. boneless skinless chicken breast, chopped
1/2 lbs. sliced mushrooms
4 large carrots, peeled and sliced
1 large yellow onion, chopped
1/3 cup almond flour
1/2 cup water
1 bay leaf
1 teaspoon fresh chopped thyme
1/4 teaspoon dried sage
Salt and pepper to taste
1 cup frozen peas
1 cup frozen green beans
1/2 cup canned coconut milk

Instructions:

1) Combine the chicken, mushrooms, carrots, and onion in the slow cooker.
2) Toss with the flour then stir in the water – add the bay leaf, sage and thyme then season with salt and pepper to taste.

3) Cover the slow cooker and cook for 7 to 8 hours on low or 4 to 5 hours on high until the chicken is cooked through.

4) Uncover the slow cooker and stir in the peas, green beans, and coconut milk.

5) Cover and cook on high heat for 5 to 10 minutes until thick. Serve hot.

Nutritional Information:

400 calories per serving, 17g fat, 18g carbs, 44.5g protein, 6g fiber

Additional Notes
Use this section to make additional notes.

_____

_____

_____

_____

_____

_____

_____

Artichoke and White Bean Ragout

Servings: 6 to 8

Ingredients:

1 tablespoon olive oil

2 large carrots, peeled and diced

4 to 5 large leeks, diced (white and light green parts only)

1 tablespoon minced garlic

2 (14.5-ounce) cans white cannellini beans, drained

1 (14.5-ounce) can diced tomatoes

2 1/2 cups chopped fennel

2 cups diced sweet potato, peeled

1 medium red pepper, cored and chopped

2 1/2 cups vegetable broth

1 (9-ounce) package frozen artichoke hearts, chopped

1 teaspoon dried basil

Salt and pepper to taste

2 to 3 cups Swiss chard, chopped

Instructions:

1) Heat the oil in a large skillet over medium heat.

2) Add the carrot, leek and garlic then cook for 5 minutes.

3) Spoon the mixture into the slow cooker and add the remaining ingredients except the Swiss chard.

4) Cover the slow cooker and cook on high heat for 8 hours until vegetables are tender.

5) Stir in the Swiss chard and cook for up to 5 minutes, until the chard is wilted.

Nutritional Information:

275 calories per serving, 3g fat, 51g carbs, 13.5g protein, 18g fiber

Additional Notes

Use this section to make additional notes.

_____

_____

_____

_____

_____

_____

Leg of Lamb with Root Vegetables

Servings: 6 to 8

Ingredients:

2 tablespoons olive oil

3 to 4 lbs. boneless leg of lamb

Salt and pepper to taste

2 lbs. sweet potato, peeled and chopped

1 large yellow onion, chopped

1 large parsnip, peeled and chopped

1 large turnip, peeled and chopped

1 large eggplant, peeled and chopped

1 cup beef broth

1 cup diced tomatoes

2 tablespoons dried rosemary

1 teaspoon dried oregano

Instructions:

Heat the oil in a large skillet over medium heat.

Season the lamb with salt and pepper to taste then add to the skillet – cook for 2 to 3 minutes per side until evenly browned.

Combine the sweet potatoes, onions, parsnips, turnips, and eggplant in the slow cooker.

Place the lamb on top of the vegetables.

Whisk together the beef broth, diced tomatoes, garlic, rosemary and oregano – pour into the slow cooker.

Cover the slow cooker and cook on low heat for 6 to 8 hours until the lamb is tender.

Nutritional Information:

500 calories per serving, 17g fat, 35g carbs, 52g protein, 8g fiber

Additional Notes
Use this section to make additional notes.

Meatless Zucchini Lasagna

Servings: 6

Ingredients:

2 teaspoons olive oil

1/2 cup diced yellow onion

1/2 small yellow squash, diced

1 clove minced garlic

Salt and pepper to taste

1/2 cup canned coconut milk, divided

1 large egg, whisked well

4 medium zucchini, sliced lengthwise into 1/4-inch slices

5 to 6 cups tomato sauce

Instructions:

1) Heat the oil in a small saucepan over medium heat.
2) To create the "cheese" sauce, stir in the onion, yellow squash, and garlic – season with salt and pepper to taste.
3) Cook for 4 minutes until the onion is translucent.
4) Whisk in 1/4 cup coconut milk and bring to a boil – reduce heat and simmer 2 minutes.

5) Remove from heat and puree the mixture using an immersion blender – blend in the rest of the coconut milk and the egg then set aside.

6) Lightly grease the insert for your slow cooker and spoon in about 1/2 cup tomato sauce.

7) Add a layer of sliced zucchini "noodles" then spoon about 1/2 cup of the cheese sauce.

8) Repeat the layers, ending with the last of the tomato sauce.

9) Cover the slow cooker and cook on high heat for 1 1/2hours.

10) Remove the lid then use a turkey baster to squeeze out the liquid pooled in the bottom of the slow cooker.

11) Heat the liquid in a saucepan over high heat – bring to a boil then simmer until thick.

12) Spoon the lasagna into bowls and drizzle with the sauce to serve.

Nutritional Information:

150 calories per serving, 8g fat, 19g carbs, 6g protein, 5.5g fiber

Braised Short Ribs with Veggies

Servings: 6 to 8

Ingredients:

2 large yellow onions, chopped

4 large carrots, peeled and chopped

3 large stalks celery, chopped

2 tablespoons olive oil

3 to 4 lbs. beef short ribs

Salt and pepper to taste

1 1/4 cups water

3/4 cups red wine vinegar

1 teaspoon chili powder

1 teaspoon dry mustard powder

1/2 teaspoon paprika

Instructions:

1) Combine the onion, carrot and celery in the slow cooker.
2) Heat the oil in a large skillet over medium-high heat.
3) Season the short ribs with salt and pepper to taste then add to the skillet.

4) Cook for 2 to 3 minutes per side until browned then add to the slow cooker on top of the vegetables.

5) Whisk together the remaining ingredients and pour into the slow cooker.

6) Cover the slow cooker and cook on low heat for 8 hours. Serve hot.

Nutritional Information:

560 calories per serving, 25g fat, 12g carbs, 67g protein, 3g fiber

Additional Notes

Use this section to make additional notes.

_____

_____

_____

_____

_____

_____

_____

DESSERT RECIPES

Apple Almond Crisp

Servings: 6 to 8

Ingredients:

6 ripe apples, peeled, cored and chopped
1 tablespoon arrowroot powder
1 tablespoon plus 1 teaspoon cinnamon, divided
1/3 cup almond flour
1/4 cup shredded unsweetened coconut
1/4 cup slivered almonds
3 tablespoons coconut oil

Instructions:

1) Spread the apples in the slow cooker and toss with arrowroot powder and 1 teaspoon cinnamon.
2) Combine the remaining ingredients in a mixing bowl until it forms a crumbled mixture.
3) Spread the mixture over the apples then cover the slow cooker.
4) Cook on low heat for 2 to 3 hours until the apples are bubbling.

Nutritional Information:

180 calories per serving, 9.5g fat, 25g carbs, 1.5g protein, 5g fiber

Additional Notes
Use this section to make additional notes.

_____

_____

_____

_____

Bananas Foster with Coconut

Servings: 8 to 10

Ingredients:

10 medium ripe bananas, peeled and quartered
1 cup unsweetened shredded coconut
1/2 cup chopped walnuts, raw
1/2 cup melted coconut oil
1/3 cup raw honey or maple syrup
1/4 cup fresh lemon juice
1 1/2 teaspoons fresh lemon zest
1 teaspoon ground cinnamon
1 teaspoon vanilla extract
Coconut cream, as needed to garnish

Instructions:

1) Arrange the bananas in a slow cooker and add the walnuts and coconut.
2) Whisk together the remaining ingredients except the coconut cream – pour over the ingredients in the slow cooker.
3) Cover and cook on low heat for 1 1/2hours until the bananas are just tender.
4) Spoon the mixture into bowls and serve drizzled with coconut cream.

Nutritional Information:

380 calories per serving, 24g fat, 44g carbs, 4g protein, 6g fiber

Additional Notes

Use this section to make additional notes.

Spiced Pumpkin Pudding

Servings: 8 to 10

Ingredients:

1 (15-ounce) can pumpkin puree

1 (12-ounce) can evaporated milk

3/4 cups coconut sugar

1/2 cup gluten-free baking mix

2 large eggs, beaten

2 tablespoons coconut oil, melted

1 1/2 teaspoons ground cinnamon

3/4 teaspoons ground nutmeg

1 tablespoon vanilla extract

Instructions:

1) Whisk together the pumpkin, evaporated milk, coconut sugar, baking mix, and eggs in a mixing bowl.
2) Beat in the coconut oil, cinnamon, nutmeg, and vanilla extract until smooth.
3) Spread the mixture in the slow cooker.
4) Cover the slow cooker and cook on low heat for 6 to 7 hours until the internal temperature reaches 160°F.
5) Cool the pudding for 10 minutes before serving.

Nutritional Information:

200 calories per serving, 7g fat, 30g carbs, 5g protein, 2g fiber

Additional Notes

Use this section to make additional notes.

_____

_____

_____

_____

_____

_____

_____

_____

_____

_____

_____

Raisin-Stuffed Baked Apples

Servings: 6

Ingredients:

6 ripe apples
1/2 cup seedless raisins
1/4 cup coconut sugar
2 tablespoons chopped walnuts
1/2 teaspoon ground cinnamon
Pinch nutmeg

Instructions:

1) Slice the tops off the apples and carefully cut out the core, leaving the bottom intact.
2) Place the apples upright in your slow cooker.
3) Combine the raisins, coconut sugar, walnuts, cinnamon and nutmeg in a mixing bowl.
4) Stuff the mixture into the apples then cover with the lid.
5) Cooke for 4 to 5 hours on low heat until the apples are tender.

Nutritional Information:

180 calories per serving, 2g fat, 43g carbs, 1.5g protein, 5g fiber

Cranberry Poached Pears

Servings: 6 to 8

Ingredients:

1 1/2 cups unsweetened cranberry juice
1/2 cup coconut sugar
1/2 cup fresh raspberries
1 tablespoon ground cinnamon
4 large ripe pears

Instructions:

1) Whisk together the cranberry juice, coconut sugar, raspberries and cinnamon in the slow cooker.
2) Peel the pears and cut them in half lengthwise – remove the cores.
3) Add the pears to the slow cooker then cover the slow cooker.
4) Cook on low heat for 4 to 5 hours until the pears are just tender.
5) Spoon the pears into dessert bowls and drizzle with the syrup to serve.

Nutritional Information:

150 calories per serving, 0g fat, 38g carbs, 0.5g protein, 5g fiber

Apple Spice Cake

Servings: 10 to 12

Ingredients:

1/2 cup coconut flour, sifted
1 cup almond flour
3 1/2 teaspoons baking powder
1 1/4 teaspoon ground cinnamon
1 teaspoon ground ginger
1/4 teaspoon salt
1/2 cup grass-fed butter, softened
1/2 cup raw honey
3 large eggs, beaten
1 cup unsweetened applesauce
2 teaspoons vanilla extract

Instructions:

Cut a piece of parchment paper to line the bottom of your slow cooker.

Whisk together the coconut flour, almond flour, baking powder, cinnamon, ginger and salt in a mixing bowl.

In another bowl, beat together the butter and honey until light.

Beat in the eggs, applesauce and vanilla extract.

Add the dry ingredients in small batches then blend smooth.

Spread the batter in the slow cooker then cover and cook for 2 to 2 1/2hours on high heat until the center is set.

Nutritional Information:

190 calories per serving, 12g fat, 20g carbs, 3g protein, 2.5g fiber

Additional Notes
Use this section to make additional notes.

_____

_____

_____

_____

_____

_____

BONUS RECIPES

Queso Verde Dip

Servings 22
Ingredients
1/2 lb uncooked ground turkey
1 tablespoon avocado oil
1 cup onion, chopped
1 8 oz vegan cream cheese
1 16 oz tomato green salsa
2 medium poblano peppers, chopped and seeded
2 cups shredded vegan Mexican cheese
1 tsp cumin, ground
1 tablespoon fresh cilantro
2 garlic cloves, minced

Instructions
Make sure you don't come into direct contact with the poblano peppers as they are hot chili peppers and can easily burn your eyes and skin. Best to wear latex gloves. Wash hands well afterwards.

Use a medium skillet and add the avocado oil.
Brown the vegan turkey along with the chopped onion.

Mix the turkey mixture with the salsa, Monterey Jack vegan cheese, cream cheese, poblano pepper, garlic, and cumin.
Use the low heat setting. Cover and cook on low for 3 to 3 1/2 hours.
Stir enough to blend the cream cheese before serving immediately.
Sprinkle with cilantro. Serve with strong tortilla chips.

Nutritional Information:

99 calories per serving, 7g fat, 5g carbs, 3g protein

Additional Notes

Use this section to make additional notes.

_____

_____

_____

_____

_____

Asparagus Breakfast Frittata

Servings 4
Ingredients:
2 cups asparagus, cooked and chopped
1 medium Roma tomato, diced
1 medium onion, diced
5 large eggs, beaten
1/4 cup almond milk
1/2 teaspoon black pepper
1/2 teaspoon sea salt

Instructions
1. Using coconut oil, lightly grease the inside of the slow cooker.
2. Add all the ingredients and mix well.
3. Cook for three hours or until done.
4. Slice into wedges and serve.

Nutritional Information:

126 calories per serving, 7g fat, 8g carbs, 10g protein

Banana-Almond Slow Cooker Oatmeal

Servings 4
Ingredients:
1 cup oats, steel cut oats
1 cup almond milk
3 cups water
2 medium bananas, sliced
2 tablespoons almond butter
1/4 teaspoon salt
2 tablespoons local honey

Instructions
1. In a 4-quart slow cooker, use cooking spray to lightly coat the inside.
2. Add water, milk, salt, and oats and combine well.
3. Cook covered for eight hours.
4. Serve one cup of cooked oatmeal into bowls and top with sliced bananas, honey, and almond butter.

Nutritional Information:

288 calories per serving, 31g fat, 52g carbs, 10g protein

Vegan Caprese Salad

This is an easy dish but you will need to cure the tofu ahead of time.

Servings 4
Ingredients:
3 vine-ripened tomatoes, cut into 1/4 inch slices
20 - 30 basil leaves, fresh
1 pkg. tofu, firm, cut into 1/4 inch slices
Olive oil, extra-virgin, enough to drizzle
Salt and pepper, coarsely ground, to taste

Instructions
1. 12 hours before prepping salad, remove tofu from container, drain and paper-towel dry.
2. Slice tofu into 1/4 inch thick pieces large enough to cover tomato slices.
3. Place a cooling rack over a lined baking sheet and arrange the tofu onto the sheet.
4. Drizzle lemon juice over both sides of tofu slices and add a dash of salt.
5. Place uncovered tofu in refrigerator for twelve hours.
6. Assemble pieces by placing tomato slices on plate and layering with tofu slices and basil.
7. Add a basil leaf in between a tomato and a slice of mozzarella cheese.
8. Layer basil leaves on top.
9. Drizzle olive oil over all the layers.
10. Salt and pepper to taste.

Nutritional Information:

241 calories per serving, 19g fat, 7g carbs, 13g protein

Additional Notes

Use this section to make additional notes.

_____

_____

_____

_____

_____

_____

_____

_____

_____

_____

_____

CONCLUSION

Slow cooking is undoubtedly a lifesaver for the busy mom who wants to ensure her family has a nutritious and delicious meal at the end of the day.

Families tend to come and go at different times, and having the ability to leave food "warming" so that family members can go to it when they need it is perfect. No more worrying that kids will dip into fast and "convenient" foods that are not necessarily good for them.

The Pegan diet is so easy and straight forward to follow. Combining it with slow cooking could not be any simpler. None of the recipes here take longer than 15 minutes to prepare, and all can be done ahead of time. Prepare them the night before, and leave them in the fridge. Then all you have to do is pop it on in the morning before you head out for your day, and it is done. It really is a match made in heaven.

Get Your Free Pegan Food Pantry Checklist

Because I know how overwhelming it can be to begin the change over to a new diet, I've prepared a quick and easy pantry food list to help you get started. You'll also receive more information, news and updates.

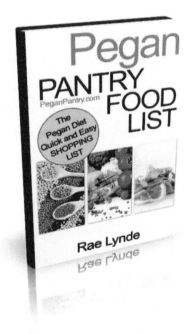

FREE PEGAN PANTRY FOOD LIST
The Pegan Diet Quick and Easy Shopping List
Go to
www.PeganPantry.com

You've Done It!

Congratulations! You've made it to the end of this cookbook. I hope this is only the beginning of an adventure for you into a whole new lifestyle with a heavy focus on healthy eating and living.

More PEGAN DIET Cookbooks

PEGAN FOR BEGINNERS
Breakfast, Lunch, and Dinner

Who doesn't love smoothies? You will love the smoothies in this book, all geared for the Pegan diet.

PEGAN SMOOTHIES
Better Health, High Energy, and Weight Loss

Enjoyed This Book?

If you enjoyed this book, would you let others know by leaving an honest review? Your review will help other potential readers discover the healthy benefits of the Pegan Diet.

You may not realize how crucial your feedback is to the success of authors like me. We are helped by those readers who have read, enjoyed, and found our books useful or helpful, and who are then happy to let others know. If you have enjoyed this book, I'd be grateful if you would take a few minutes to leave a review on Amazon.

To leave a review, go to:

Amazon.com/author/RaeLynde

If your book did not come from Amazon.com, please go to the appropriate country website.

Thank you!

Rae Lynde

ABOUT RAE LYNDE

Like my Pegan Pantry Facebook Page:
https://www.facebook.com/PeganPantry

Rae Lynde loves food, enjoys cooking, and loves to find ways to combine good food and good health. When she's not in the kitchen or pouring over recipe books, she's reading and gardening. She enjoys growing her own herbs and vegetables, too.

Follow me on Amazon:
Amazon.com/author/RaeLynde

NOTES

_____

_____

_____

_____

_____

_____

_____

_____

_____

_____

_____

_____

_____

_____

INDEX